55 days

EVERYDAY

POETRY & ART

SWAGATA NAIK

ISBN
Paperback 979-8-89556-844-6
Hardcase 979-8-89610-672-2

CONTENTS

AUTHOR'S NOTE

I have been writing since I was I was 12, or even earlier than that because I was writing letters to my parents. No matter where my life was, the words never left my side. They were my refuge and my release. Now they are here for you. As you read through these, you might wonder what kind of person wrote them. Or the purpose or the meaning behind them. However, as the author, what I am hoping would be fulfilling for you, is finding your own meaning behind these words. Even if it is just a feeling or the fragment of one, I hope you find it in any of the words or brush strokes.

In my pursuit of these crazy words and colours, my heart found support all along the way. I had excellent teachers, and some who taught me to be excellent. I had encouragement from friends and colleagues. I cannot name all the authors who came before me and have given me this gift. But there are those who I would like to name here.

My father, Shrikanta, who has made all of this possible and who said only one thing my entire life - I support you no matter what. My mother, Jyoti who gave me the sense of real beauty, something that is reflected in the work here. My aunt, Monika who got me my first book and without whom I would not be who I am. My brother, Suraj who taught me several lessons that too find their release in the words.

My first and only boss Zia Mody, and my mentor as a lawyer, Nikhil Sakhardande who sharpened me as a person and a professional at the highest level.

My assistant, Sanjay without whom, neither I nor my three kids, Casper, Shifu and Hershey would have an organised home or life. My kids who have given me the love that only they can have in their unconditional hearts and furry paws.

My ex husband, Vikramjit, without whom I would not have several memories and sensibilities that inspired the words or the art.

My friend Zinia who pushed me to put my art out there every single day since the day we met, with the most innovative ideas and tender intelligence. My friend Kashyap who together with Zinia is my family in this vibrant city, and has inspired me as an artist through all means possible. It was way back in April of 2024, Kashyap told me to put my poems out in the world.

The final person I would like to thank is myself for everything. Well done kid!

Lastly, a note about the title. It was suggested by Kashyap one fine evening after we had spent 55 days seeing Baldev, his father, tirelessly contend for life. Witnessing Baldev Uncle's journey taught me the beauty and the impermanence of life, and the strength and the finality of death. The book is titled in honour of the love and life I saw in those 55 transformative days.

And most of all, thank YOU, for reading and spending time with me. I hope you find the heart and the life in these pages that are so dear to me.

— Swagata

1. IT IS YOU ISN'T IT?

I lay my head against the cold tile and heard us.

I tugged at you, asking, walking in a daze behind those flimsy doors,

Our only protectors, the lone warriors of love as we close our eyes to let each fibre feel what our hearts feel in that moment,

The love, the want and the bravery of it all.

My hands look for you in your body,

I feel you searching me,

Singing a different song,

Compelling me to know it's beat,

I wonder then, if I am compelled enough.

Are you?

I wonder, are you where I am,

Is it necessary that you be there too,

No it is not.

You are in the same mountains as I am, and that is enough,

You are on the same journey as I am, and that is enough,

It is you though, isn't it?

Not just the starry fog in my dreams that I pretend is you?

It is you isn't it?

A little forward, a little lost, a little dazed but on the same mountain, in the same pool, near the same valley,

You on the same journey as I am.

As I lay my head on the cold tile, I hear you.

Yes, yes I am. I would like this hill very much.

2. SO ALIVE!

I saw it even as it came to life,

Even as he put his pen to paper to bring me to life,

Even as the artist came throbbing and alive,

And even as the man peeled off each layer from every side.

I saw it even as the White turned black and blue and grey,

Even as the White was beaten and turned black and blue,

Even as the White saw its reflection and it's oh so pristine silver grey hue,

Even as the blue stood royally against a black awning stage

And even as the man bleated and artist
fled from White screens to its true grey
age.

I saw even as the thorns turned into a
religion,

Even as the belated followers came to
the dead musician,

Even as the tunes survived and brushed
the pristine aside,

Even as each pore and each breath came
to life,

And even as he put pen to paper to make
the rainbow dancers and the gypsy winds
alive, alive and oh so alive.

3. THE HEROES

She was at the station,

in her frayed clothes and mismatched

shoes singing for some coins,

and her mind kept asking -

will the legends please stand up.

He was smaller than the rest and that

made it easier fro him.

His customers were desperate.

And yet as he saw each junkie, he

wondered

when the legends would show up.

She kept fixing the buckle on a new shoe

while her mother sniffled in the seat

next to her.

As she looked at the school building approaching,

she wondered would she ever meet a legend.

He cycled along the dusty road with tears flowing,

his tie a little askew, shirt buttons broken,

as he clutched the perfect mark-sheet.

As he entered his colony,

and saw his father take off his helmet,

he hid his beat up face, and wondered

would a legend ever come through there.

She and he found each other sleeping

on either side of the highway.

A different She sat up doing her homework

While a different He fixed the chain on his cycle.

They in their dreams of sleep,

And they in their dreams while awake,

Found themselves next to a pink lake.

They stood there, Hope yet in their ages.

As their different feet,

touched the familiar edge of the water.

One by one.

That's when the legends showed up.

4. IF I COULD...

If by the sheer will of my gaze i could

Make your heart happy i would

If by looking at you i could

make the dew seem not like tears but
magic, i would

if by not saying anything i could

make you know how your downcast eyes
make me die, i would

if by picking your gaze and turning it
to the moon i could

turn you from the night in your heart,
i would

if by looking at your hand i could

take it in mine and clasp it hard, i
would

if by sighing at the sight of your hair
i could

stroke it and blow away your troubles
i would

if by not taking my eyes off your fingers
i could

kiss them and make you smile i would

if by worrying whether you would look
back, i could

make you know i want you too, i would

if by thinking i would give anything to
brighten your day i could

give away everything precious to get
your smile, i would

if by praying and hoping i could

make all your hopes come true i would

if by looking at your face i could

make all those prayers bless your head,
i would

if by wishing for it i could

get back anything you have lost i would

if by the sheer will of my gaze, if by
looking, i could

wipe those tears, i would

5. THE CITY

This city that fights with its salty coast everyday, it has a certain sweetness to it,

This world that extends from south to the north embodies several worlds in it.

Sometimes you feel like catching it,

And sometimes just playing with it.

Sometimes you feel like becoming a child,

And sometimes you feel like getting lost in the infinite depths of those aged waves.

Come on O traveller, let's talk to those waves.

Come on, O Observer, let's measure the transparent boundaries of this city without knowing it or introducing ourselves to it.

6. THE LITTLE FLEAS

It should remain rather clean, exclaimed the flea.

But it is not, exclaimed her brother.

How do they live?

These all powerful creatures of nature.

Definitely, not clean.

What about all the lather in the soap?

Before they meet the most desired of companions.

Well, it still does not clean the all important nethers, does it?

Oh, I wish they would shed some light right over here.

After all that expense and a little bit of credit.

I really do wish they would treat us as the true companions we are.

Ah! Must we jump to another, exclaimed little flea to her brother.

Let's hope that is cleaner than the carrier of this cheap lavender.

7. NOBODY WANTS TO DANCE WITH ME

They see the ribbons tied.

And they see the eyebrows unpried.

They see the face closed.

And they see the hands not quite posed.

They hear the cool note.

And they hear the heavy silence as if by rote.

They hear the frowned denial unreachable even by boat.

And they hear every syllable of an inexplicable negative vote.

They do not hear the pulsating heart,

Or the sweaty hands.

They do not see the pile of discarded clothes,

Or the mixed up rubber bands.

They do not see the conversations rehearsed,

Or the letters written in verse.

They would not hear, that were it the right voice, it would be a yes.

They would not see, that winds would flow across oceans, were it the right universe.

8. THE HOPE OF YOU

It is so compelling to get lost in the universe that is you,

And yet not want a shred of what is you,

Or maybe this madness is a version of control over my own universe,

Because otherwise all I am, is lost in the want- the hope of you.

9. GRATITUDE

Tucked away in gratitude.

A small loaf of bread.

But of course, it was not paid for.

And yet the gratitude was there in her running feet.

Little hands, clutching a little reminder of the big hunger.

The gloved gun looking away graciously.

The Olive trees shedding their shade to offer some free glee.

The cross on her arm was hard to bear.

And yet the bread made her smile so fair.

The feet found the sand, not the best playmate.

And yet the wheat made her heart inflate.

The eyes stung with the harsh sun.

And yet the hope of a morsel brought tears of joys more than one.

Her skin had burnt from the salt in the air.

And yet, as he bit into the precious share of his,

She laughed and cried, and tucked her little brother's hair.

With all the gratitude that filled her little heart and alert mind,

Under that sun, beneath the olives while playing in all the sand they could find.

10. DREAD

It filled me with dread.

The unending words on life's unstopping screen.

While my words boiled on paper.

The words filled me with dread.

The vicious circles of what should have been.

While the pain in me, feels the swirling ether.

The thoughts filled me with dread.

The unending spirals of imagined dangers careen.

While my heart tries to find the sharp end of the scissor.

My hands fill me with dread.

The, should I should I not makes me question What must it mean?

While my Soul attempts yet again to Divine, a lesson in the obscure letter.

11. THE ARMOURS AND STARDUST

They were beautiful.

Broken. Put together with stardust.

The chinks in their armours were all the more beautiful for it.

And yet they were armours.

The heavy ones. The ones you cannot see.

But they look bedazzling to those of us who can see.

Almost overwhelming.

The armours housed light.

Carefully hidden, protected light.

Sometimes they betrayed themselves and twinkled like stars.

Sometimes the light was hidden so far inside that you could not touch it.

The tragedy was that the stardust didn't know when the light would be hidden.

It would bring its hopeful fingers to its breast and sometimes feel the light beating.

Much like a heart.

And sometimes feel its fingers caress emptiness.

It knew it wasn't its fault. But it was stardust.

As fleeting and twinkling as the stars above.

And it was housed in those heavy armours. The beautiful, tentative ones.

Its bounden duty was to feel the light.

For, if it could not, how could anyone see the dust?

So it tried.

Sometimes it hoped, another set of fingers would help.

But most times, it was by itself.

Today though, was different.

Another set of fingers had found their way.

It was another armour. Another stardust, another hidden light.

And today, it was happy.

It shut its ears when the armours clanged.

But it was happy.

Because it could entangle its fingers into another set.

Oh! It just put its fingers on its breast.

That light! That light feels so different. So warm. So cold.

Shall I help? It asked.

The new stardust smiled and let it in.

Let the armours breathe.

Today our fingers find each other.

They find each other's light.

Today we are beautiful.

And they knew.

Every day they were together.

They would be beautiful.

12. THE AUTOBIOGRAPHY OF A GOD

What would the autobiography of a God sound like?

Is a God even the right term for him? her? it?

If it is in all and all are in it,

Then would it even be an autobiography?

Would the eyes be fair?

Would the sight be impartial?

Would a world of sorrow simply be the scales of mundane justice?

Would laughter and joy be of little consequence?

Or would a community simply be a bunch of unaware followers?

Would it be right to call it anything other than an autobiography?

When each of the leaves and particle and being is the God?

When each sound and wail and laughter belongs to the omnipresent?

When each colour and texture and sensation comes together to make it infinite?

And yet the question remains.

What would the autobiography of a God sound like?

Perhaps the whole universe.

Or perhaps the tiniest neuron in your pure heart.

Who knows?

And who can ever know?

13. FLAMES

Sometimes the flames catch and sometimes they don't,

The matchbox that is my heart sputters out in the wind.

While sometimes the flames catch,

and sometimes they don't.

The tinder box that remains as tightly closed as my soul loses its lonely spark,

While sometimes the flames catch,

and sometimes they don't.

You hold all of my breath while life drains out of me,

While sometimes the flames catch,

and sometimes they don't.

A whirlwind of envy and rage possesses my very being,

As finally the flames catch,

only to die out a few momentous moments later.

14. THE FOREST

The roots find warm arms to intertwine with,

While the branches sway in their own wind.

The dry parchments find their own company,

While the new leaves open in their own little nook.

The flowers find their decay in hoards,

While buds must come forth

one petal after the next, all by its lone self.

Can I find my very own arms, the branches cried.

I would like to see another sunny face, said the new leaf.

My petals would like to kiss some other
petals.

But don't they already?

Said the ageing all seeing wind while

the sun echoed its sagely laughter.

Look, it is the soft embrace of

that new leaf that protects you, dear
bud.

The erratic swaying of the lonesome
branch

that births you dear leaf.

That new bloom and the budding leaf

make you beautiful, oh mighty branch.

But it isn't quite the same, is it?

Rose the relentless lament.

Is it not? And so on and so forth

the unending dialogue went?

15. THE COSMIC CONSPIRACY

The cosmos conspired to give him what he desired the most.

A slap to that magnificent ego.

A resounding kick to a narcissistic sense of purpose.

A crack at an insulated sense of virtue.

A prick to the righteous illusion of a kind heart.

Yes, it was the cosmos that conspired.

To give him exactly what he needed.

It was the cosmos after all.

The all knowing omnipresent medley of atoms.

The one that keeps the delicate balance in what we call our beloved world.

The one that balances the biggest desires in the smallest needs.

And it fails to fulfil that need and the desire when it teeters, the most.

The cosmos conspired, yes.

But it did not conspire enough.

And it did not conspire enough for each creature, walking its tenuous membranes.

Those with the egos and the virtues, and those that never deserved the cosmos to begin with.

16. SHADOWS

The shadows on the pavement dance as the shadows on my leg,

As the feet march across it, so does your flighty heart's last dreg.

Why so many feet, you say.

Why such little heart, I say?

Those feet do not only march, they dance too.

That heart doesn't love, but the shadows do.

17. MISTAKEN IDENTITY

They call me a witch.

But I do not like spindles.

That is not me but the usurper in the west with the itch.

I, for one, I am very discerning of baubles.

They call me the ice queen.

But I do not enjoy mirrors.

That is not me, but the costumed wrinkled had-been.

I, for one, would rather spend my time with ink and papers.

They call me the wicked one.

Gah! I do not like baked children.

That one is the senile fool with a barely working oven.

I, for one, am a stout vegetarian.

They call me villainous and evil and moody.

But I do like a talking head fastened securely to the neck.

That one is heartless and filled with envy.

I can neither be her nor the others for I am a rather virtuous wreck.

18. THE BUS DRIVER

An unseeing wave of gratitude.

Is that what he heard?

As he transported the millieu and the herd.

A mumbled pleasantry.

Is that what he saw?

As he sat day after day in a box filled with passengers caught in life's maw.

A loud expletive.

Now that he is familiar with.

As his bus goes up, down and in a maze much like an Indian myth.

19. CENTAURUS

He is bound to be barbaric, isn't he?

The all knowing universe looked at me
with no measure of pity,

The pristine stars with their puritan
lineage would not be bothered to even
sneer at me.

Yet I found my own nomadic corners,

And I found my own set of steps out of
the impunity and arrogance guaranteed
in the blood of my brothers,

While I ignored the doubt that in my
heart flutters.

In my pursuit of healing and wisdom, I
carved out a pulpit of peace,

In my pursuit of belonging, I bled at my stiff knees,

And in my pursuit of a salute, I charted the most hostile of seas.

In this generous dark sky, I, Chiron, have no place at its celestial table,

In the delighted notes of the natives, mine is but a long drawn incomprehensible, foreign fable.

Among the starry hues of my father's heavenly ocean, my matted gold finds no label.

I do not flee my lot in this mercurial universe.

I study and teach all that my mind gathers.

And I continue to bandage those heroes that come to me in familiar tatters.

As I sat one unknowing day, in contemplation of my crucible in which severe flames prance.

A jubilant arrow bit at my heels, singing fortune's tricky dance.

As I looked upon an Unhealing wound, I wondered if this was my legacy's disguised chance.

I did not yet scream in my pain.

I sat in contemplation, but this time of immortality's gain.

And I looked upon Prometheus, a hero, tied up in an unending chain not for doing something heroic, but humane.

Perhaps my redemption lies in taking over that fine man's punishment.

Perhaps my final act of absolution may be to take over a thankless task that any other hero may lament.

And perhaps this creature that never quite belonged may yet find a purpose in another's hubris even without any armament.

As I surrendered myself to the thrall
of a bartered fate,

I feel a light surround me as I ascend
to become a punished inmate.

The universe that looks upon me smiles as
I finally become a design of consequence
on its decorated gate.

Bound to shine in acceptance and piety.

Not quite the barbarian, and yet with
no family or fealty.

He is bound to be an immortal, isn't
he?

20. THE SINGER ON THE STREET

The pebbles under my feet keep rhythm.

Of what you ask?

Why, of my songs of course.

Or maybe of the laughter of my ever seeking cracked steps.

Perhaps of the rumbles of emptiness in the heart of me, the artist.

Or more likely the unlimited dreams I see in the mirages on the hot road.

But most definitely of the wonder I create in those that see me from their towers way above.

The pebbles under my feet keep rhythm.

As you, my friend in the tower, in
your wonder, don't see my cracked feet
beneath the colours of my heart parading
with the songs of my life.

21. THE THOUGHT OF YOU

For the very thought of you makes me clasp my hand.

For the mere glimpse of you makes my thoughts fall apart,

like a tree split apart for a magic wand,

like a bird hushed away at the start of dawn.

For the very thought of you makes my heart tremble.

For the mere mention of you in my heart makes it run wild.

Like a dancers feet even as they fumble,

Like a dew drop in flight.

A thought, a name, a mention and a glimpse so sudden.

A dance, a magic, an irregular motion of a heart so hidden.

22. SMUDGED LIPS

The smudges on the lip tell stories.

Of?

Of mirrors witnessing unabashed trilling love.

Of windows glancing through a flown dove.

The stroke on the glass recounts memories.

Of?

Of frames sighing over cracked cloth in teal.

Of chalices touched but just beyond reveal.

The faded colour under the cloth hums histories.

Of?

Of boxes dancing to broken notes.

Of figurines swaying to kaleidoscopic rotes.

23. THE SOFT MEMBRANE

The membrane is too soft.

It may burst.

It is pumping too quickly.

But it is only a flutter.

It has not burst yet.

It may still spill over.

It is too fast.

But can it not be handled with some water?

Not this time. Maybe, no.

Why? It has survived thus far.

It hurts too much.

But it is only the smallest matter.

Maybe.

Maybe it is.

Maybe it will survive.

But what if, the walls, the membrane gets softer.

Why? What then?

24. THE SOUL'S FRAGMENTS

The soul's fragments dart within marshes of oil and water.

They are asking for an address.

They are asking for a badge for their ceremonial dress.

They are looking for binding light.

The marshes balk at the hint of any blinding fight.

The soul's fragments slake their thirst on kind varnish.

Coated & protected, they warm their fingers on the bank.

Watching the reeds count their rank.

They watch as the marshes count them
too with wise nods and faces long.

Not daring to ask themselves - was this
the address all along?

25. WHERE?

Where might you be hidden?

In the Olive leaves?

Or the gauze bandaging the tiny feet?

Where might you be found?

In the deserts of holy lands?

Or the pits of despair between unmarked graves?

Where might you live?

Not in a place, I tentatively, but joyously called home.

Not in the rooms, where a stroke of a pen would slash my infants' hearts.

Where might you be reborn?

In a place where the Samaritan finds the way.

Under a sky, where the walls of greed do not have much say

26. SUYODHAN'S LAMENT

Let me open their eyes! My soul screamed!
Let me open their eyes!

My broken body stared up at the roof of
the forest, I remembered her eyes.

But in my delirium I saw the stalwart's
eyes.

As I stood there being accused by a
gluttonous bully's lies.

But as always in just silence, his
bright eyes looked away.

Today, prone on a bed of arrows, his
bright eyes shed tears as only they
may.

In righteousness and honour and failure
as clear as day.

He had seen my heart break in as many pieces as the number of soldiers on that wasteland lay.

I had been happy. I had been young. So young.

My embrace held only love as the shadow of inevitable history around us hung.

I could not stop loving her even now, as the toll on my destiny was rung.

And I could not forgive her as long as there was even one breath in my torn lung.

The audience knew who was the better wrestler all those moons ago.

The audience knew too who was the better archer and the bigger man all those moons ago.

The radiant benefactor would give up a kingdom for me.

The resplendent challenger who was mocked by that august company.

The beautiful creature who I anointed as King because who deserved better!

The resilient friend for whom, I missed the confusion germinating in that tender heart in her.

She had found the thwarted dark prince's sagging shoulders.

Did she think that birth and caste were relevant to a man's worth.

I never saw another dark prince's delicate manoeuvering.

After that day maybe I never saw anything else but the sun's scorned princeling.

She left with her brother.

And I would not hear from her.

But she was mine.

And I had not anticipated that fated trine.

"She is married now…

They…they eloped on a chariot and there is futility in any row."

I stood there as sweat dripped down my quivering soul.

"Who drove the chariot Sir?" I asked, hoping for an absolution of her role.

It was she. She drove it, Son.

I bowed my head and lifted my head to the ubiquitous sun.

She…she chose him. And I choose……I choose to respect her choice.

As I said this with no quiver in my voice,

I saw her laughter.

And my eyes found solace in shedding no salt or water.

I lie maimed and my spirit ravaged by a necessary war.

And yet remember that heartbreak and who all that love was for.

I wish I had opened my eyes then.

I wish I had opened them and seen the web of fate then.

The heartbreak was inevitable.

My defeat was inevitable.

My promises were inevitable.

Her breaking them was inevitable.

I wish I had opened my eyes then.

And I wish it wasn't her riding that chariot then.

And I wish…

27. TO THOSE WE CALL PETS

They sat facing opposites.

Not quite knowing the fate at the end of their own wrists.

Their noses faced different directions and smelled different flavours.

Not quite knowing the fulfilment that linger at the end of the common mirth.

Their fur coats showed different colours of joy and happiness.

Their kind eyes were the same in soothing with kindness.

Some might see the nails at the end of those enthusiastic paws.

All I see are my friends who come to greet me as if I would be their greatest loss.

They wake up as I write - a trio of
unplanned fate.

They come to me with enthusiasm even as
I touch heaven's gate.

The round, the tall, the dark, all one
in their unconditional love.

With their unassuming shortlived
dedication and adoration in the gruff.

28. YOU

It is the language of the soul.

That gets shrouded in your own mystery.

It is the song of the Divine

That gets inundated as your childhood quietly bows out.

It is the symphony of nature.

That hides under our concrete wishes.

It is the design of the universe.

That finds its steps covered under the mud of your distrust.

It is the flow of your voice

That gets buried under your fingers, tapping away into nothingness.

And yet it is the hope of life

That peaks its head out from under all
that trouble and all that brush,

That whispers and laughs softly to
remind you of the love

and gentle force that is all you.

29. POLITE REVELRY

There is such politeness in your drunken revelry.

While the heads get dragged on our luxury.

There is such blindness in our shiny relations.

While small hands suffer from cracked dreams.

There is such courtesy in your divisive apolitics.

While trudging feet, try to make democratic choices.

There is such tepidness in your definition of culture.

While eyes with true discernment contend with convenient artifice.

There is a fools garden on lavish stages
of our ill spent fortunes.

While ill fed bodies and ill fed hearts,
follow the fireworks with hopes of some
of that vaporising light and fading
tunes.

30. WHO DO I WRITE FOR?

Who do I write for?

For a million reflections of me in a thousand possible worlds.

For a million reflections of us in a hundred impossible worlds.

For a million friends of a million me.

For a million foes that look and feel like you.

Who do I recite for?

For the millions of me who are deaf to what I would like to say.

For a million others who are blind to the way hearts beat.

For a million more dreamers sleep walking in the thousand worlds and times in which you do not write nor recite.

Who do I dance for?

Isn't that quite clear by now?

Oh, for my million hearts and my million breaks.

For my obscure identities and my known loves.

And most of all for the one heart that may never quite find you in a million worlds.

31. MEMORIES

I've not written in a long time.

It hurts to put ink to paper for such a tragic mime.

Hell it hurts to even breathe without catching my breath.

It hurts to even catch my breath.

My heart aches and I don't know what that might mean.

I wish the blood would stop flowing and become a had been.

If only the warm memories would dry up my tears.

If only I didn't have a cold bed to ward off my fears.

Its tough to be a piece of a star.

Its so so tough to just be a piece of a star.

It hurts to be on an orbit in a vein.

It hurts to be only on the orbit in vain.

With not a single touch nor a single whisper.

With not half a smile nor the memory of a caress like feather.

With not a kiss nor an embrace of love.

Memories. Memories. Memories and only memories beloved.

32. GREATER THAN DEATH

Her love was greater than death.

Or was it?

Her love was beaten around the mountain of excess.

While duty for profit, desecrated, all the virtue of the hapless.

Her love roamed the groves of contempt unwittingly.

While gold cuffed pens killed off the innocent boldly.

Her love looked for the sanctuary of nutrition and joy.

While honey tipped barbs, continue to take away her children down to the smallest boy.

Her love looked to meet her union in the corridors with a warm warm embrace.

While deceit laced each word dropped from a beautiful face.

Her love did not appear much greater than death.

As her equal's heart went cold, and the infant's lips drew its last breath.

33. THE ZODIAC

The fish swam in the opposite directions.

While the bearer poured his rebellion into their peaceful waters.

The hooves climbed the beloved mountains of even more beloved toil.

While the archer took aim at the joyous sky.

The stings smarted in the forbidden cave's depths.

While the scales found their beautiful imbalance in their airy quest.

The maiden carries a sheaf of preciseness and perfect grains.

While the lion roar in its glorious pride.

The feet find their sideways path on the sands of love.

While the many faces look to the many directions of a mercurial life.

The horns pointed true north in unflinching resolve.

While the god of war locked in a martial push to start the starry cycle in a difficult bid to evolve.

34. THE LAST OF ME

As I sat, loving, losing and loving again.

The wind beat my heart and curdled my brain.

As I stood up remembering his pain.

The wind sighed and left my wicked heart.

As I looked at the empty roof and the sky beyond.

The sun blinded me and shut me away.

As I shifted my gaze to the barren around.

The sun sighed and left my treacherous mind.

As I lost my thoughts in the depths of my greed.

The ocean drowned my mind and sound.

As I bent to recover my fleeting thought.

The ocean sighed and receded from my flailing soul.

As I ran to save my body from its unforgiving longing.

The sand sucked in my feet and caught me in a spell.

And as I lay there dying.

The sand sighed engulfing me in its folds.

The last of me and my very end.

35. I LOVE YOU

I don't know why. And I certainly do not know how.

But I love you, and I have never loved you as right now.

For I crave a touch and a warm caress.

A cold rain pouring and us dancing with our hair amess.

I crave the tattoo that my heart plays as I see you.

As I see a familiar lovely you.

I crave the taboo that my mind wags its sagely head at.

Even as I make love to you with no heed to when or whereat.

And right now, I hate you and I hate me.

For why would I let myself love you
only in memory.

Why would you let me fall so deep that
I cannot even breathe.

Why would you I let you let me fall so
enmeshed that I will never breathe.

Enmeshed and fallen. Sooted in heaven.

But never a moment with you and never
a fortune so craven.

A breath. All I crave is a breath for
my parched heart.

A length. All I need is a length of
rope longer than the one suffocating my
bound heart.

It eludes me. And it eludes my ever
thinning faith.

You elude me and your love eludes my
ever falling embrace.

Even as my breath goes and my heart
dies,

I love you as I have never loved you
through all our tides.

36. THE IMAGINARY FRIEND

He ran in glee.

His Messiah was here in his overweight glory.

He screamed in joy.

His benefactor grunted as he did, when he was a boy.

He yelled his demands.

His jolly friend counted them on his hands.

He jumped on his merry belly.

His trusted magician caught him, and he missed rarely.

He cuddled under the massive umbrella with the accompanying sun.

His friend's magnanimous arm sheltered him and the sun, as though they were one.

He would soon cease to remember the curious giant from his imaginary reams.

While his friend would continue to find the laughing boy, even in the darkest of dreams.

37. STRANGERS IN NAME

And here we are, strangers in name and unknown in thought.

And here we go,

Bound in tears and connected with inexplicable dots.

And here we remain,

Clasped in pain and clutching at forgotten straws.

And here we stay,

Risen in devotion and possessed with each other's flaws.

38. I AM A MOTHER

I am a mother in a lot of ways.

I am a mourner on most days.

I also am a rebel.

I am a mendicant in this worldly court, reduced to grovel.

I am allowed to protect.

Only when there is no ego standing cruelly erect.

I am a mother, not by choice, but by love.

I am a soldier, not by choice, but because of a knife in a velvet glove.

I also am an undesired warrior.

In a world, where the likes take away the heart and leave it hollow, but merrier.

I am a mother without the lifeboat of laughter.

In the waters of my infants' blood, I am even a reluctant swimmer.

The three headed dog of myth, probably overjoys, my child with mirth.

While I curse the prophets that denied me the joy of my unfortunate birth.

39. MY COMPANION'S EYES

Your eyes look at me with an unconditional mirror.

Your eyes talk to me through an unwavering, lack of veneer.

Your eyes do not blink at my glorious failings.

Your eyes welcome me through my grievous wailings.

Your eyes put a smile on my comedic face.

Your eyes put a joyous balloon in my unfeeling human brace.

Your eyes do not stare, they look.

Could I perhaps find a more interesting book?

Your eyes are my refuge at the end of the road.

Your eyes are my comfort at the end of the lost leaders board.

Your eyes are doused in the Divine.

And oh my beautiful companion, how can I call them just mine?

40. THE ERRANT ARROW

It glided smoothly in the distance.

As my heart shattered into a million intents.

It shown its own light on the tracks.

As the pieces lay on the ground writhing in dissent.

It had broken me and run its course.

While the pieces cried, seeking elusive pity, and lament.

It came from a place, unknown.

As I am left wondering, while my little hearts mourn.

It vanished artfully into a void of mischief all its own.

While the remnants of my soul plead for the grace which had all but flown.

I do not understand its purpose or role,

Save that it made me less and yet somehow whole.

41. IT IS STRANGE

It is strange to feel love for a pair of pattering feet,

Belonging to a stumbling thought not yet complete.

In a lane of falling rain and dark shadow,

Those little feet with almost burnt candle flow.

You would want to kiss the bare neck,

Taking upon the rain at your call and beck.

To give your lone kind a respite

And calm your anxious besides.

It would bring the image of a smile, a half complete raise of the eyebrow,

Or it would bring the sound of a laugh or vision of tomorrow.

Softly it would whisper on your sleepy mind.

And wake you into a dream with consciousness behind.

It is strange to feel love at knuckles on your window.

Rapping away to catch your gaze and turn it to the meadow.

The knuckles on the hands of a fleeting moment.

Maybe a hidden pleasure or a faded lament.

In a lane of falling rain and dark shadow,

Those exquisite hands with meaningful fingers flow.

Brushing dust off tomorrow and colouring today.

Catching and presenting to you an orange ray.

It is strange to feel love at the loveliest song,

That the wind may sing even if not for long.

And you are lost in that lane of shadow and of falling rain.

Not quite comprehending but seeing the smoke on the train.

And you are lost on the shadow of the horizon

As it lightly falls removing the memory of the sun.

42. THE MOON WAITS

As the moon looks upon the still lit up dusk,

It knows not that it fights with the formidable sun and it's dying rays,

It knows not that except for a lone pair of eyes, none notice it's beautiful ways.

It's reflected light has not washed over even more formidable stars of the night yet,

It's silvery protection has not enamoured those that it seeks to have met.

It merely looks on, even as the sun saunters on to the other side.

It merely waits, even as the universe
is unaware of its impending embrace and

As it makes unbeknownst love to the
formidable stars on their worldly ride.

43. THE GOSSAMER GRACE OF GRIEF

The gossamer grace of being surrounded by your loved fears.

The quiet sighs of a helpless partner of many years.

The world milling about you, as if nothing is in tears.

The wind singing its song of every day, loud and so clear.

It seems like an ordinary day to almost everyone, but you.

Or perhaps it is not ordinary to anyone, but you.

You sit there, praying as that old one in the last pew.

You depart giving way to the young ones
far and few.

It takes much effort to remove that
gossamer of grace.

It takes much effort to look upon that
familiar face.

It does not take much effort for life to
disappear without a trace.

It really does not take much effort for
love to yet find itself without its
living base.

44. UNSAID ASSASSINS

The knives cut deep, dark and desolate much like bad dreams.

The papers display their own unending cruelties.

The barbs snigger as they find the unaware tendons.

The claws patiently picked at unseeing eyes.

The glass shards refracted the skin as they did light.

The thorns had their own story as they sternly protected their flowers.

The nails hammered with loud expletives and ugly splotches.

And while each of these found their material pleasure,

The words ruled over them all, in glory and beyond any measure.

They cut in cruelty.

They sniggered in their injuries stealthily.

They refracted a dozen meanings with even two of their stern sentinels.

And the unsaid assassins haughtily looked on,

while the hammer, the nails, the shards, the knives, the thorns and the claws

found their reparable marks in harmless bushels.

45. OBLIVION

How beautifully oblivious are we to the
moments that make us this fragile,

How beautifully unaware are we of the
moments even when they happen,

How beautifully blind are we to our
heart being broken

or a warm friendship being struck,

How beautifully incomplete are we as
that heart breaks

and that friendship holds us in its
warm incomplete embrace.

46. LIFE'S RATION

Her cotton drape was frayed now.

His mesh cap didn't have uniform patterns.

They had laughed together in a time when there was what they called peace.

Companions amidst many an olivine crease.

The missing marble was clutched in his hand.

The ungifted scarf she made was fluttering on the abandoned mantle.

As the world around them exploded with greed and meaningless ambition.

They hid in their favourite hiding place, not knowing they were out of life's ration.

47. REACH FOR BETTER

We live in different houses.

We live in different cities within the
same city.

We see a different sky.

We watch a different moon in the same
city.

But we take the same train.

Walk the same roads.

Feel the same sweat on our brow.

Same angst in our guts.

On the same train, we have different
seats.

You see, some of us get late.

Some of us start early.

Some of us stay on track.

And some of us ask for help.

We see different things.

Our experiences are different.

But we take the same train.

And stay on our chosen path.

We might start at different points.

But we aim to reach the same place.

A place above ours.

A place in the stars.

You might not be taking that train now.

But it is never too late.

To get on that train.

To start, to see the stars you want reach for.

To keep reaching and to Reach For Better.

48. THE WINGS OF THE BUTTERFLY

It flutters in the wind.

Cocooned within its tenuous membranes.

The delicate silk of its life bringing
it to completion.

It grows in almost rains.

Peeking from behind its uncertain wings.

The purple screens of its dreams pushing
it to the first of many flights.

It laughs in the uncertain weathers.

Open and now facing its short beautiful
existence.

The veined lines of it's already lived
wishes drawing rainbows in the sky.

49. THE VOID

Unlike in the void, the scream echoed in the mountains.

Unlike in the void, the song bubbled merrily on the stream.

Unlike in the void, the sun shone with a thousand new colours.

Unlike in the void, the butterfly wings found the wind.

Unlike in the void, the flowers bloomed to their pristine ordinariness.

Unlike in the void, her laughter resonated next to the trees.

Unlike in the void, the rainbows collided for the pieces of the sky.

Unlike in the void, the lovers found the warmth of their hands on the bridge.

Unlike in the void, each life, big or
small, grand or mediocre, lived to its
glorious end daily.

50. WHAT I WANT...

I want to breathe your air.

I want to see the sun through your hair.

I want to smell the roses in your hand.

I want to walk the feet on this land.

I want to see the rainbows, blinding your eyes.

I want to find the wrinkles as you scan the skies.

I want to feel your lovers with your warm embrace.

I want to feel the sun's fire on your cold face.

I want to taste the crystal on your tongue.

I want to feel the blood drain through your lung.

I want to see the meanders in your heart.

I want to sense the rejuvenation in your stomach for your art.

I want to feel each particle of who you are.

And I want to hear each of those syllables that do not travel far.

I want to be you as you are me.

And I want to be me in love with you, but free.

51. HOW DO YOU FEEL?

I do not know how to feel fear.

When I unfold the abandoned flag

Or when I decide that the colour of rebellion is the right one to smear.

I do not know how to express sadness.

When I liked one of a million candles on the unsafe streets.

Or when I find the scales of justice, make a mess.

I do not know how to show the weakness in my heart.

When I walk at the shields and the unthinking helmets.

Or when my eyes sting with gases meant to subdue humanity's revolutionary chart.

I do not know how the empath finds the right pulse.

Because I find it hard to find my own tears.

Or find the heartbreak, amidst all the fears.

52. THE OFFENDING SYNTAX

Are those spellings that Hard?

Is the syntax only for a bard?

Must it defile the beauty of a well structured thought.

A delicately constructed plot.

Must it be so hard to add the right or the precise Sound?

A scythe to a model creation rarely found.

How do you sleep with an abbreviation under the pillow?

When a fully formed set of syllables would rightly comfort you to a truly sleepy hollow.

How do you not see the discordant dissonance?

While the perfection behind an elegant set of sounds, would sound like the obscure heavens.

How do you not hear the shrillness much worse than that of a mythical banshee or a mermaid?

When a sentence at the height of its careful evolution may soothe every soul, whether enraged or afraid.

Are those spellings really that hard?

And must peace lie only in the diaries of a bard?

53. A LOVE LOST

Have you ever felt alone and joyful in a crowd?

An earnest nod, a languid smile, perhaps a sliver of unbound joy found.

Laughing eyes, dancing feet, an aching smiling heart.

Unfeeling hunting eyes, trudging shimmering soul, an artistically upset apple cart.

Have you ever felt a full heart in a crowd?

A love lost, and the lost love found.

54. CROW'S FEET

The birth of a crow's feet is something of a mystery.

As the eyes well up a tiny crease forms.

As the lips laugh, the crease deepens.

As the sun is harsh, the crease finds colour.

As the children die, the creases wail at the horror.

As the hunger persists the creases are met by unfortunate frowns.

As the children are killed, the frowns meet the crow's feet.

The birth of those feet are met by hollowed eyes in some parts of the world.

As the eyes well up, the laughs quieten,
the sun brightens, and the children
die.

The mystery of the crows feet remains
unresolved.

55. THEY CALL ME A CHURCH

They called me a church, and then they bombed me.

They had made all of those inert stones into something picturesque and dreamy.

They took the glass stained with care before I was tainted.

They took the beautiful bombarded pews, added with love after I was painted.

I cried in agony as everything around me burned.

I cried in ignorance, as my kingly past, had been fortuitously, turned

The air in me grew heavy because the doors remained locked

The god in me grew weary of being resurrected because the strength of stones used to create me were mocked

In time and love the map grew around me.

In strength and hope the jagged steps around me, gracefully withdrew.

I was always just a building - and yet a monument in the relentless sun and rain.

I was always a refuge - so common, and yet a witness to immeasurable devotion, and pain.

I did not in my lifetime personally, offer platitudes, and consolations,

While the necessary war and nature kept causing inevitable destructions.

They had no choice, but to loose their weapons and tools of a grand plan.

I had no choice, but to lose each of my stones, set in an obeisant trance by the hands of man.

I was always the church, the marker of the rich life of each devotee.

They were always the power, the makers of my walls, so decorated and mighty.

I lay in ruin, and they wailed at my decimated bowels.

I wondered in those ruins if nature had for me any of its marvels.

And it did open one of its oldest and enduring miracles for me.

While the city built around me and around waylaid pillars of unspoken piety,

Each of my witnesses came to cherish my desolate wounds as a beloved dream

And each of those bent heads, and tears lifted me into something that was unexpectedly supreme.

The city was shiny and the roads paved with perfect lines.

While I lay there in cherished memories in aggrieved, but tenderly loving minds.

They call me a church and true enough, there are ruins and records of my death.

But they took all of those torn shrouds
and gave me life as gentle and tender
as the daily bloom of a baby's breath.

www.ingramcontent.com/pod-product-compliance
Lightning Source LLC
Chambersburg PA
CBHW040908110726

48005CB00006B/835